For
the Living
and
the Dead

ALSO BY TOMAS TRANSTRÖMER

Selected Poems 1954–1986

For
the Living
and
the Dead

New Poems and a Memoir

TOMAS TRANSTRÖMER

Edited by DANIEL HALPERN

Translated by Joanna Bankier, Robert Bly,
Samuel Charters, Robin Fulton, and Malena Mörling

THE ECCO PRESS

The Ecco Press
100 West Broad Street
Hopewell, New Jersey 08525

Published simultaneously in Canada
by Penguin Books Canada Ltd., Ontario

Printed in the United States of America

Designed by Barbara Cohen Aronica

Library of Congress Cataloging-in-Publication Data
Tranströmer, Tomas, 1931–
For the living and the dead : new poems and a memoir / Tomas Tranströmer ;
translated by Joanna Bankier . . . [et al.]. —1st ed.
p.   cm.
Translated from Swedish.
ISBN 0-88001-436-9
I. Tranströmer, Tomas, 1931– —Biography.
I. Bankier, Joanna.   II. Title.
PT9876.3.R3Z465   1996
839.71'74 – – dc20   95-21742

The text of this book is set in Weiss.

9 8 7 6 5 4 3 2 1

FIRST EDITION

CONTENTS

I

II

III

The names listed are the translators

EDITORIAL NOTE

The poems in this collection come to us from a variety of hands. Samuel Charters, Joanna Bankier, Robert Bly, and Robin Fulton have for many years translated the work of Tomas Tranströmer into English. I have also included a number of translations by Malena Mörling, a young Swedish-born poet who has recently joined the group of translators working with the important poetry of Tranströmer.

In 1987, The Ecco Press published *Selected Poems*, edited by Robert Hass, whose introduction addresses the difficulties of a project such as the one at hand. He wrote, "I undertook the job, qualified by my ignorance of Swedish. It turned out to be a little less simple than it might have seemed. There were often three or four translations of a poem available, each with its own virtue." As editor of *For the Living and the Dead*, I made my selection from the various worthy versions—which existed for each of the poems included here—to arrive at a collection that is unified and readable in English, according to my sense of the poems as a *book*. Four of the poems in this collection appeared in *Selected Poems*, under "New Poems"—although for this edition I have used Samuel Charters' version of "The Forgotten Captain" and Robert Bly's version of "Vermeer."

I wish to thank all the translators for their ongoing work in the service of Tranströmer and his English-language readers, and The Swedish Academy, for their generous support. I especially want to thank Robert Hass, whose suggestions, ongoing support, and enthusiasm made the publication of this book possible.

—DANIEL HALPERN

I

THE FORGOTTEN CAPTAIN

We have many shadows. I was on the way home
in the September night when Y
climbed out of his grave after forty years
and kept me company.

At first he was entirely empty, only a name,
but his thoughts swam
faster than the time ran
and caught up to us.

I put his eyes to mine and saw
the sea in wartime.
The last boat he commanded
grew beneath us.

The ships of the Atlantic convoy crept before and behind,
the ones that would survive
and the ones that had been given The Mark
(invisible to everyone)

while the sleepless nights relieved each other
but never him.
The life jacket sat under the oil skin.
He never came home.

He bled to death from an inner weeping
in a hospital in Cardiff.
He finally got to lie down
and turn into horizon.

Goodbye eleven knot convoys! Goodbye 1940!
Here ends the history of the world.
The bombing planes were left hanging.
The heaths bloomed.

The photo from the turn of the century shows a beach.
Standing there are six dressed up boys.
They have sailboats in their arms.
What serious expressions!

The boats that become life and death for some of them.
And to write about the dead
is also a game that gets heavy
with what is to come.

STREETS IN SHANGHAI

I

Many in the park are reading the white butterfly.
I love that cabbage butterfly as if it were a fluttering corner of truth itself!

At dawn the running crowds set our silent planet going.
Then the park fills with people. For each one eight faces polished like jade,
    for all situations, to avoid mistakes.

For each one also the invisible face that reflects "something you don't talk
    about."
Something that emerges in tired moments and is as pungent as a sip of
    Viper schnapps, with its lingering, scaly aftertaste.

The carp in the pond are always moving, they swim while they sleep,
    they are an example for the faithful: always in motion.

II

Now it's noon. The washing flutters in the gray sea wind high above the
    cyclists
who come in tight shoals. Notice the labyrinths to the sides!

I am surrounded by written characters I can't interpret. I am illiterate
    through and through.
But I have paid what I'm supposed to and have receipts for everything. I
    have gathered so many unreadable receipts.
I am an old tree with withered leaves that hang on and can't fall to earth.

And a gust from the sea rustles all these receipts.

III

At dawn the trudging crowds set our silent planet going.
We're all on board the street, it's as crowded as the deck of a ferry.
Where are we going? Are there enough teacups? We can consider ourselves
    fortunate for boarding on this street in time!
It's a thousand years before the birth of claustrophobia.

Behind each one walking here hovers a cross that wants to catch up to us,
pass us, join us.
Something that wants to sneak up on us from behind and cover our eyes
    and whisper, "Guess who?"

We look almost happy out in the sun, while we bleed to death from wounds
    we know nothing about.

THE NIGHTINGALE IN BADELUNDA

In the green midnight at the nightingale's northern limit. Heavy leaves hang in trance, the deaf cars race towards the neon-line. The nightingale's voice rises without wavering to the side, it's as penetrating as a cock-crow, but beautiful and free of vanity. I was in prison and it visited me. I was sick and it visited me. I didn't notice it then, but I do now. Time streams down from the sun and the moon and into all the tick-tock-thankful clocks. But right here there is no time. Only the nightingale's voice, the raw resonant notes that whet the night sky's gleaming scythe.

BERCEUSE

I am a mummy at rest in the blue coffin of the forests, in the perpetual roar
of engines and rubber and asphalt.

What happened during the day sinks, the lessons are heavier than life.

The wheelbarrow rolled forward on its single wheel and I myself travelled
on my spinning psyche, but now my thoughts have stopped going
round and the wheelbarrow has got wings.

At long last, when space is black, a plane will come. The passengers will see
the cities beneath them glittering like the gold of the Goths.

DEEP IN EUROPE

I am a dark hull floating between two lock-gates
rest in the hotel bed while the city around me wakens.
The silent clamor and the grey light stream in
and raise me slowly to the next level: the morning.

Overhead horizon. They want to say something, the dead.
They smoke but don't eat, they don't breathe but they keep their voice.
I'll be hurrying through the streets as one of them.
The blackened cathedral, heavy as a moon causes ebb and flow.

SIX WINTERS

I

A child sleeps in the black hotel.
And just outside: the winter night
where the wide-eyed dice roll.

II

An elite of the dead turned to stone
in Katarina cemetery
where the wind shakes in its armor from Svalbard.

III

One winter during the war when I was sick
an enormous icicle grew outside the window.
Neighbor and harpoon, memory without explanation.

IV

Ice hangs down from the edge of the roof.
Icicles: the upside down Gothic.
Abstract cattle, glass udders.

V

An empty railroad car on a spur.
Calm. Heraldic.
With the journeys in its claws.

VI

Snow flurries tonight, moonlight. The moonlight
jellyfish itself floats before us. Our smiles
on the way home. Bewitched avenue.

ROMANESQUE ARCHES

The tourists are crowded into the enormous Romanesque church in the half
    darkness.
Vault gaping behind vault and no overview.
Some candle flames fluttered.
A faceless angel embraced me
and whispered through my whole body:
"Don't be ashamed that you're a human being, be proud!
Within you vaults open endlessly behind vaults.
You'll never be completed, and that's as it should be."
I was blind with tears
and I was driven out into the sun seething piazza
along with Mr. and Mrs. Jones, Herr Tanaka, and Signora Sabatini
and within each of them vaults opened endlessly behind vaults.

EPIGRAM

The buildings of capital, hives of the killer bees,
                    honey for the few.
He served there. But in a dark tunnel he unfolded his wings
and flew when no-one was looking. He had to live his life again.

FEMALE PORTRAIT, 19TH CENTURY

Her voice is stifled in the clothing. Her eyes
follow the gladiator. Then she herself is
on the arena. Is she free? A gilt frame
                    strangles the picture.

MOTIFS FROM THE MIDDLE AGES

Under our fascinating facial expressions the skull
is always waiting, the poker face. While
the sun slowly rolls across the sky.
                    The chess game goes on.

A sound of barber's scissors from the thicket.
The sun rolls slowly across the sky.
The chess game ends in a draw. In
                    the silence of the rainbow.

MADRIGAL

I inherited a dark forest where I seldom walk. But a day is coming when the living and the dead change places. Then the forest starts moving. We aren't without hope. The worst crime remains unsolved despite the efforts of many police. In the same way there is a great unsolved love in our lives. I inherited a dark forest, but today I am walking in the other forest, the light one. And the living things that sing, wiggle, wave and crawl! It's spring and the air is very strong. I have an examination at the University of Forgetfullness and am as emptyhanded as the shirt on the clothesline.

THE KINGDOM OF UNCERTAINTY

The bureau chief leans forward and draws an X
and her earrings sway like the sword of Damocles.

As a mottled butterfly becomes invisible against the ground
the demon merges with the opened newspaper.

A helmet worn by no one has taken power.
The mother turtle escapes flying under the water.

EARLY MAY STANZAS

A May wood. The invisible removal load,
   my whole life, like a haunting here. Birds in song.
      In the silent pools, midge-larvae—
         their dancing furious question-marks.

I escape to the same places, and the same words.
    Cool sea breeze. And the ice-dragon licks the back
      of my neck while sunlight blazes.
        The load is burning with chilly flames.

SILENCE

Walk past, they are buried . .
A cloud glides over the disc of sun.

Starvation is a tall building
that moves around at night

in the bedroom the dark staff of the
elevator shaft opens toward the spaces within.

Flowers in the ditch. Fanfare and silence.
Walk past, they are buried . .

The table silver survives in large shoals
in the great depths where the Atlantic is black.

GOLDEN WASP

The blindworm that legless lizard flows along the porch step
calm and majestic as an anaconda, only the size is different.
The sky is covered with clouds but the sun pushes through.
That kind of day.

This morning she who is dear to me drove away the evil spirits.
As when you open the door of a dark shed somewhere in the south
and the light pours in
and the cockroaches dart off into the corners and up the walls
and are gone—you saw them and you didn't see them—
so her nakedness made the demons run.

As if they never existed.
But they'll come back.
With a thousand hands crossing the lines in the old-fashioned telephone
        exchange of the nerves.

It's the fifth of July. The lupins are stretching up as if
        they wanted to catch sight of the sea.
We're in the church of keeping-silence, in the piety according to no letter.
As if they didn't exist, the implacable faces of the patriarchs
and the misspelling of God's name in stone.

I saw a true-to-the-letter TV preacher who'd piled in the money.
But he was weak now and needed the support of a bodyguard,
who was a well-tailored young man with a smile tight as a muzzle.
A smile stifling a scream.
The scream of a child left alone in a hospital bed when the parents leave.

The divine brushes against a human being and lights a flame
but then draws back.
Why?
The flame attracts the shadows, they fly rustling in and join the flame,
which rises and blackens. And the smoke spreads out black and strangling.
At last only the black smoke, at last only the pious executioner.

The pious executioner leans forward
over the market-place and the crowd that make a grainy mirror
where he can see himself.

The greatest fanatic is the greatest doubter. Without knowing it.
He is a pact between two
where the one is a hundred per cent visible
and the other invisible.
How I hate that expression "a hundred per cent."

Those who can never exist anywhere except on their facades
those who are never absent-minded
those who never open the wrong door and catch a glimpse of the
        Unidentified One.
Walk past them!

It's the fifth of July. The sky is covered with clouds but the sun pushes
        through.
The blindworm flows along the porch step, calm and majestic
                as an anaconda.
The blindworm as if there were no bureaucracy.
The golden wasp as if there were no idolatry.
The lupins as if there were no "hundred per cent."

I know the depth where one is both prisoner and ruler, like Persephone.
I often lay in the stiff grass down there
and saw the earth arch over me.
The vault of the earth.

Often—that's half my life.

But today my gaze has left me.
My blindness has gone away.
The dark bat has left my face and is scissoring around in summer's
                bright space.

GRIEF GONDOLA No. 2

I

Two old guys, father-in-law and son-in-law, Liszt and Wagner live on the
    Grand Canal
along with that nervous woman who is wife to King Midas—
I mean the one who turns everyone he touches into Wagner.
The green cold of the ocean presses upward through the palazzo floor.
Wagner has received the Mark, his famous Punchinello profile sags now
his face is a white flag.
The heavily loaded gondola carries their lives, two return tickets and a one-way.

II

A palazzo window blows open; they make a face at the sudden draft.
Outside on the water the garbage gondola passes, oared by two one-armed thieves.
Liszt has composed a few chords so heavy one should send them
off to the Institute for Mineralogical Studies in Padua.
Meteorites!
Far too heavy to stay where they are, they start sinking and sinking down
    through the coming years until they reach
the year of the Brownshirts.
The heavily loaded gondola carried the hunched stones of the future.

III

Pinholes toward 1990.

March 25: Disturbed about Lithuania.
I dreamt that I visited a large hospital.
No doctors. Everyone was a patient.

In the same dream a newborn baby girl
who spoke in complete sentences.

IV

The son-in-law, comparatively, is a modernist, Liszt is a moth-eaten grandsigneur.
It's a disguise.
The deep that tries and throws away various masks has chosen this particular
    mask for him—
the deep that loves to invade humanity without showing its own face.

V

Old father Liszt is used to lugging his own bags through storm, snow, and heat
and when he arrives at death no one will meet him at the station.
A warm whiff of a highly cultured cognac carried him off in the middle of a
    commision.
He always has commisions.
Two thousand letters a year!
The schoolboy who has to write the misspelled word a hundred times before
    he can go home.
The heavily loaded gondola carries life, it is simple and black.

VI

Back now to 1990.

I dreamt I drove a hundred miles for nothing.
Then everything got huge. Sparrows the size of hens
sang so loud that my ears closed up.

I dreamt that I had sketched piano keys out
on the kitchen table. I played on them, without a sound.
Neighbors came by to listen.

VII

The clavier which has been silent through the entire *Parsifal* (of course it
    was listening) finally gets to talk.
Sighs . . . sospiri . . .
When Liszt plays tonight he holds down the seapedal so that the ocean's
    green force
rises through the floor and penetrates every stone of the building.
Good evening to you, beautiful deep!
The heavily loaded gondola carries life, it is simple and black.

VIII

I dreamt that I was to start school but arrived late.
Everyone in the room wore white masks on their faces.
It was impossible to know which was the teacher.

(Note: *During late 1882 and early 1883, Liszt visited his daughter Cosima and her husband
Richard Wagner in Venice. Wagner died several months later. Liszt's two piano pieces published
under the title* Grief Gondola *were composed during that time.*)

II

Memories Look at Me:
A Memoir

MEMORIES

"My life." Thinking these words, I see before me a streak of light. On closer inspection it has the form of a comet, with head and tail. The brightest end, the head, is childhood and growing up. The nucleus, the densest part, is infancy, that first period, in which the most important features of our life are determined. I try to remember, I try to penetrate there. But it is difficult to move in these concentrated regions, it is dangerous, it feels as if I am coming close to death itself. Further back, the comet thins out—that's the longer part, the tail. It becomes more and more sparse, but also broader. I am now far out in the comet's tail; I am sixty as I write this.

Our earliest experiences are for the most part inaccessible. Retellings, memories of memories, reconstructions based on moods that suddenly flare into life.

My earliest datable memory is a feeling. A feeling of pride. I have just turned three and it has been declared that this is very significant, that I am now big. I'm in bed in a bright room, then clamber down to the floor stunningly aware of the fact that I am becoming a grown-up. I have a doll to whom I gave the most beautiful name I could think of: Karin Spinna. I don't treat her in a motherly fashion. She is more like a comrade or someone I am in love with.

We live in Stockholm, in the Söder area, at Swedenborgsgatan 33 (now called Grindsgatan). Father is still part of the family but is soon to leave. Our ways are quite "modern"—right from the start I use the familiar "du" form to my parents. My mother's parents are close by, just round the corner, in Blekingegatan.

My maternal grandfather, Carl Helmer Westerberg, was born in 1860. He was a ship's pilot and a very good friend of mine, seventy-one years older than myself. Oddly enough, there was the same difference in age between him and his own maternal grandfather, who was born in 1789: the storming of the Bastille, the Anjala mutiny, Mozart writing his clarinet quintet. Two equal steps back in time, two long steps, yet not really so very long. We can touch history.

Grandfather's way of speech belonged to the nineteenth century. Many of his expressions would today seem surprisingly old-fashioned. But in his mouth, and to my ear, they felt altogether natural. He was a fairly short man, with a white moustache and a prominent and rather crooked nose—"like a Turk's," as he said. His temperament was lively and he could flare up. His occasional outbursts were never taken too seriously and they were over as soon as they had begun. He was quite without aggression of the insistent kind. Indeed he was so conciliatory that he risked being labelled as soft. He wanted to keep on the best side even of people who might be criticized—in their absence—in the course of ordinary conversation. "But surely you must agree that X is a crook!" "Well, well—that's something I don't really know about . . ."

After the divorce, mother and I moved to Folkungagatan 57, a lower-middle-class tenement. A motley crowd lived there in close proximity to each other. My memories of life there arrange themselves like scenes from a film of the thirties or the forties, with the appropriate list of characters. The lovable concierge, her strong laconic husband whom I admired because, among other things, he had been poisoned by gas and that suggested a heroic closeness to dangerous machines.

There was a trickle of comers and goers who didn't belong there. The occasional drunk would slowly return to his wits on the stairway. Several times a week beggars would ring. They would stand there in the porch mumbling. Mother made sandwiches for them—she gave them slices of bread rather than money.

We lived on the fifth floor. At the top, that is. There were four doors, plus the entry to the attic. On one of them was the name Orke, press photographer. In a way it seemed grand to live beside a press photographer.

Our immediate neighbour, the one we heard through the wall, was a bachelor, well into middle age, yellowish complexion. He worked at home, running some sort of broker's business by phone. In the course of his calls he often gave vent to hilarious guffaws that burst through the walls into our flat.

Another recurring sound was the pop of corks. Beer bottles did not have metal caps then. Those Dionysiac sounds, the guffaws of laughter and the popping of corks, seemed hardly to belong to the spectrally pale old fellow sometimes met in the lift. As the years passed he became suspicious and the bouts of laughter diminished in frequency.

Once there was an outbreak of violence. I was quite small. A neighbour had been shut out by his wife; he was drunk and furious and she had barricaded herself in. He tried to break down the door and bawled out various threats. What I remember is that he screamed the peculiar sentence: "I don't give a damn if I go to Kungsholmen!" I asked mother what he meant, about Kungsholmen. She explained that the police headquarters was there. And that part of town then acquired a sense of something fearful. (That was a feeling intensified when I visited St. Erik's Hospital and saw the war-wounded from Finland who were cared for there in the winter of 1939–40.)

Mother left for work early in the morning. She didn't take a tram or bus—throughout her entire adult life she walked to and fro between Söder and Östermalm—she worked in the Hedvig Leonora School and was in charge of the third and fourth classes year after year. She was a devoted teacher and greatly involved with the children. One might imagine it would be hard for her to accept retirement. But it wasn't—she felt greatly relieved.

Since mother worked we had a home-help, a "maid" as she was called, though "child-minder" would have been nearer the truth. She slept in a minimal room which was really part of the kitchen and which was not included in the official flat-with-two-rooms-and-kitchen designation of our home.

When I was five or six, our maid was called Anna-Lisa and she came from Eslöv, in Skåne in the south of Sweden. I thought she was very attractive: blond frizzy hair, a turned-up nose, a mild Skåne accent. She was a lovely person and I still feel something special when I pass Eslöv station. But I have never actually stepped off the train at that magic place.

She was particularly talented at drawing. Disney figures were her specialty. I myself drew almost uninterruptedly throughout those years, in the late 1930s. Grandfather brought home rolls of brown paper of the sort then used in all the grocery shops, and I filled the sheets with illustrated stories. I had, to be sure, taught myself to write at the age of five. But it was too slow a process. My imagination needed some speedier means of expression. I didn't even have enough patience to draw properly. I developed a kind of shorthand sketching method with figures in violent movement, breakneck drama yet no details. Cartoon strips consumed only by myself.

One day in the mid-1930s I disappeared in the middle of Stockholm. Mother and I had been to a school concert. In the crush by the exit I lost my grasp of her hand. I was carried helplessly away by the human current and since I was so small I could not be discovered. Darkness was falling over Hötorget. I stood there, robbed of all sense of security. There were people all around me but they were intent on their own business. There was nothing to hold on to. It was my first experience of death.

After an initial period of panic I began to think. It should be possible to walk home. It was absolutely possible. We had come by bus. I had knelt on the seat as I usually did and looked out of the bus window. Drottninggatan had flowed past. What I had to do now, simply, was to walk back the same way, bus stop by bus stop.

I went in the right direction. Of that long walk I have a clear memory of only one part—of reaching Norrbro and seeing the water under the bridge. The traffic here was heavy and I didn't dare set off across the street. I turned to a man who was standing beside me and said: "There's a lot of traffic here." He took me by the hand and led me across.

But then he let go of me. I don't know why this man and all the other un-known adults thought it was quite in order for a little boy to wander by him-self through Stockholm on a dark evening. But that's how it was. The remain-der of the journey—through Gamla Stan, the old town, over Slussen and into Söder—must have been complicated. Perhaps I homed in on my destination with the help of the same mysterious compass that dogs and carrier pigeons have in them—no matter where they are released they always find the way home. I remember nothing of that part. Well, yes, I do—I remember how my self-confidence grew and grew so that when I did at last arrive home I was quite euphoric. Grandfather met me. My devastated mother was sitting in the police station following the progress of the search for me. Grandfather's firm nerves didn't fail him; he received me quite naturally. He was glad of course, but didn't make a fuss. It all felt secure and natural.

MUSEUMS

As a child I was attracted to museums. First, the Natural History Museum. What a building! Gigantic, Babylonian, inexhaustible! On the ground floor, hall after hall where stuffed mammals and birds thronged in the dust. And the arches, smelling of bones, where the whales hung from the roof. Then one floor up: the fossils, the invertebrates . . .

I was taken to the Natural History Museum when I was only about five years old. At the entrance, two elephant skeletons met the visitor. They were the two guardians at the gateway to the miraculous. They made an overwhelming impression on me and I drew them in a big sketchbook.

After a time those visits to the Natural History Museum stopped. I was going through a phase when I was quite terrified of skeletons. The worst was the bony figure depicted at the end of the article on "Man" in the Nordic Family Lexicon. But my fear was aroused by skeletons in general, including the elephant skeletons at the entrance to the museum. I became frightened even of my own drawing of them and couldn't bring myself to open the sketchbook.

My interest now turned to the Railway Museum. Nowadays it occupies spacious premises just outside the town of Gävle but then the entire museum was squeezed into a part of the district of Klara right in the centre of Stockholm. Twice a week grandfather and I made our way down from Söder and visited the museum. Grandfather must himself have been enthralled by the model trains, otherwise he would hardly have endured so many visits. When we decided to make a day of it we would finish up in Stockholm Central Station, which was nearby, and watch the trains come steaming in, full-sized.

The museum staff noticed the zeal of the young boy and on one occasion I was taken into the museum office and allowed to write my name (with a back-to-front S) in a visitors' book. I wanted to be a railway engineer. I was, however, more interested in steam engines than in electric ones. In other words, I was more romantic than technical.

Some time later, as a schoolboy, I returned to the Natural History Museum. I was now an amateur zoologist, solemn, like a little professor. I sat bent over the books about insects and fish.

I had started my own collections. They were kept at home in a cupboard. But inside my skull there grew up an immense museum and a kind of interplay developed between this imaginary one and the very real one which I visited.

I went out to the Natural History Museum more or less every second Sunday. I took the tram to Roslagstull and walked the rest. The road was always a little longer than I had imagined. I remember those foot marches very clearly: it was always windy, my nose ran, my eyes filled with tears. I don't remember the journeys in the opposite direction. It's as if I never went home, only out to the museum, a sniffling, tearful, hopeful expedition towards a giant Babylonian building.

Finally arriving, I would be greeted by the elephant skeletons. I often went directly to the "old" part, with animals which had been stuffed away back in the eighteenth century, some of them rather clumsily prepared, with swollen heads. Yet there was a special magic there. Big artificial landscapes with elegantly designed and positioned animal models failed to catch my interest—they were make-believe, something for children. No, it had to be quite clear that this was not a matter of living animals. They were stuffed, they stood there in the service of science. The scientific method I was closest to was the Linnean: discover, collect, examine.

I would work through the museum. Long pauses among the whales and in the paleontology rooms. And then the part which detained me most of all: the invertebrates.

I never had any contact with other visitors. In fact, I don't remember there being other visitors at all. Other museums which I occasionally visited—the National Maritime Museum, the National Museum of Ethnography, the Museum of Technology—were always crowded. But the Natural History Museum seemed to stay open only for me.

One day I did encounter someone—no, not a visitor, he was a professor or something like that—working in the museum. We met among the invertebrates—he suddenly materialized between the showcases, and was almost as small in stature as I was. He spoke half to himself. At once we were involved in a discussion of mollusks. He was so absent-minded or so unprejudiced that he treated me like an adult. One of those guardian angels who appeared now and then in my childhood and touched me with its wings.

Our conversation resulted in my being allowed into a section of the museum that was not open to the public. I was given much good advice on the preparation of small animals, and was equipped with little glass tubes which seemed to me truly professional.

I collected insects, above all beetles, from the age of eleven until I turned fifteen. Then other, competing, interests, mostly artistic, forced their attentions on me. How melancholy it felt, that entomology must give way! I convinced myself that this was only a temporary adjustment. In fifty years or so I would resume my collecting.

The activity began in the spring and then flourished of course in the summer, out on the island of Runmarö. In the summerhouse, where we had little enough space to move around in, there stood jam jars with dead insects and a display board for butterflies. And lingering everywhere: the smell of ethyl acetate, a smell I carried with me since I always had a tin of the insect killer in my pocket.

It would no doubt have been more daring to use potassium cyanide as the handbook recommended. Fortunately that substance was not within my reach and so I never had to test my courage by choosing whether or not to use it.

Many were involved in the insect hunt. The neighbourhood children learnt to sound the alarm when they saw some insect that could be of interest. "Here's one!" echoed among the houses, and I would come rushing along with the butterfly net.

I was out on endless expeditions. A life in the open air without the slightest thought of thereby improving my health. I had no aesthetic opinions on my booty, of course—this was, after all, Science—but I absorbed unawares many experiences of natural beauty. I moved in the great mystery. I learnt that the ground was alive, that there was an infinite world of creeping and flying things living their own rich life without paying the least regard to us.

I caught a fraction of a fraction of that world and pinned it down in my boxes, which I still have. A hidden mini-museum of which I am seldom conscious. But they're sitting there, those insects. As if they were biding their time.

PRIMARY SCHOOL

I began in Katarina Norra Primary School and my teacher was Miss R, a tidy spinster who changed her clothes every day. As school ended each Saturday, each child was given a caramel, but otherwise she was often strict. She was generous when it came to pulling hair and delivering blows, although she never hit me. I was the son of a teacher.

My chief task that first term was to sit still at my desk. I could already write and count. I was allowed to sit and cut out shapes in coloured paper, but what the shapes were I can't remember.

I have a feeling that the atmosphere was fairly good throughout my first year there but that it chilled somewhat as time passed. Any disturbance to good order, any hitches or snags, made Miss R lose her temper. We were not allowed to be restless or loud-voiced. We were not to whine. We were not to experience unexpected difficulties in learning something. Above all, we were not to do *anything* unexpected. Any little child who wet himself or herself in shame and fear could hope for no mercy.

As I said, being the son of a teacher saved me from blows. But I could feel the oppressive atmosphere generated by all those threats and reproaches. In the background there was always the head teacher, a hawk-nosed dangerous character. The very worst prospect was to be sent to a reform school, something which would be mentioned on special occasions. I never felt this as a threat to me personally but the very idea gave a disagreeable sensation.

I could well imagine what a reformatory was like, the more so since I'd heard the name of one—"Skrubba" ("Scrub"), a name suggesting rasps and planes. I took it as self-evident that the inmates were subjected to daily torture. The world view which I had acquired allowed for the existence of special institutions where adults tortured children—perhaps to death—for having been noisy. That was dreadful, but so must it be. If we were noisy, then . . .

When a boy from our school was taken to a reformatory and then returned after a year there, I regarded him as someone who had risen from the dead.

A more realistic threat was evacuation. During the first year of the war, plans were made for the evacuation of all schoolchildren from the bigger cities. Mother wrote the name TRANSTRÖMER with marking ink on our sheets and so on. The question was whether I would be evacuated with mother and her school class or with my own class from Katarina Norra, i.e., deported with Miss R. I suspected the latter.

I escaped evacuation. Life at school went on. I spent all my time in school longing for the day to come to an end so that I could throw myself into what really interested me: Africa, the underwater world, the Middle Ages, etc. The only thing which really caught my attention in school was the wall charts. I was a devotee of wall charts. My greatest happiness was to accompany teacher to the storeroom to fetch some worn cardboard chart. While doing so I could peep at the other ones hanging there. I tried to make some at home, as best I could.

One important difference between my life and that of my classmates was that I could not produce any father. The majority of my class came from working-class families where divorce was clearly something very rare. I would never admit that there was anything peculiar about my domestic situation. Not even to myself. No, of course I had a father, even if I met him only once a year (usually on Christmas Eve), and I kept track of him—at one point during the war he was, for example, on a torpedo boat and he sent me an amusing letter. I would have liked to have shown this letter in class but the right chance never came.

I remember a moment of panic. I had been absent for a couple of days and when I came back a classmate told me that the teacher—not Miss R but a substitute—had said to the class that they must not tease me on account of the fact that I had no father. In other words, they were sorry for me. I panicked, hearing that. I was obviously abnormal. I tried to talk it all away, my face bright red.

I was acutely aware of the danger of being regarded as an outsider because at heart I suspected I was one. I was absorbed in interests which no normal boy would have. I joined a drawing class, voluntarily, and sketched underwater scenes: fish, sea urchins, crabs, shells. Teacher remarked out loud that my drawings were very "special" and my panic returned. There was a kind of insensitive adult who always wanted to point me out as somehow odd. My classmates were really more tolerant. I was neither popular nor bullied.

Hasse, a big darkish boy who was five times stronger than I was, had a habit of wrestling with me every break during our first year at school. At first I resisted violently but that got me nowhere for he just put me to the ground anyway and triumphed over me. At last I thought up a way of disappointing him: total relaxation. When he approached me I pretended that my Real Self had flown away leaving only a corpse behind, a lifeless rag which he could press to the ground as he wished. He soon grew tired of that.

I wonder what this method of turning myself into a lifeless rag can have meant for me further on in life. The art of being ridden roughshod over while yet maintaining one's self-respect. Have I resorted to the trick too often? Sometimes it works, sometimes not.

THE WAR

It was the spring of 1940. I was a skinny nine-year-old stooped over the newspaper, intent on the war map where black arrows indicated the advance of the German tank divisions. Those arrows penetrated France and for us, Hitler's enemies, they lived as parasites in our bodies. I really counted myself as one of Hitler's enemies. My political engagement has never been so wholehearted!

To write of the political engagement of a nine-year-old no doubt invites derision, but this was hardly a question of politics in the proper sense of the word. I hadn't the slightest conception of matters such as social problems, classes, trade unions, the economy, the distribution of resources, the rival claims of socialism and capitalism. A "Communist" was someone who supported Russia. "Right-wing" was a shady term because some of those at that end of the political spectrum had German leanings. My further understanding of "Right-wing" was that one voted in that direction if one were rich. Yet what did it really mean to be rich? On a few occasions we were invited for a meal with a family who were described as rich. They lived in Äppelviken and the master of the house was a wholesale dealer. A large villa, servants in black and white. I noticed that the boy in the family—he was my age—had an incredibly big toy car, a fire engine, highly desirable. How did one get hold of such a thing? I had a momentary glimpse of the idea that the family belonged to a different social class, one in which people could afford unusually large toy cars. That is still an isolated and not very important memory.

Another memory: during a visit home with a classmate it surprised me that there was no WC, only a dry closet out in the backyard, like the kind we had in the country. We would pee into a discarded saucepan which my friend's mother would swill down the kitchen sink. It was picturesque detail. On the whole it didn't occur to me that the family lacked this or that. And the villa in Äppelvik did not strike me as remarkable. I was far short of the capacity which many seem to have acquired even in their early years of grasping the class status and economic level of a given environment merely at a glance. Many children seemed able to do so, not I.

My "political" instincts were directed entirely at the war and Nazism. I believed one was either a Nazi or an anti-Nazi. I had no understanding of that lukewarm attitude, that opportunistic wait-and-see stance which was widespread in Sweden. I interpreted that either as support for the Allies or as covert Nazism. When I realized that some person I liked was really "pro-German," I immediately felt a terrible tightening over my breast. Everything was ruined. There could never be any kind of fellow feeling between us.

From those close to me I expected unequivocal support. One evening when we were on a visit to Uncle Elof and Aunt Agda, the news inspired my generally taciturn uncle to comment that "the English are successfully retreating . . ." He said this almost with regret yet it struck me there was an ironic undertone (on the whole irony was foreign to him) and I suddenly felt that tightening. The Allied version of history was never questioned. I stared grimly up at the roof light. There was consolation to be found there. It had the shape of a British steel helmet: like a soup plate.

On Sundays we often had dinner in Enskede with my other uncle and aunt on Mother's side; they provided a sort of support family for Mother after the divorce. It was part of the ritual there to turn on the BBC's Swedish broadcast on the radio. I shall never forget the programme's opening flourish: first the victory signal and then the signature tune, which was alleged to be "Purcell's Trumpet Voluntary" but which in fact was a rather puffed-up arrangement of a harpsichord piece by Jeremiah Clarke. The announcer's calm voice, with a shade of accent, spoke directly to me from a world of friendly heroes who saw to it that it was business as usual even if bombs were raining down.

When we were on the suburban train on the way to Enskede I always wanted Mother—who hated attracting attention—to unfold the propaganda paper *News from Great Britain*, and thus silently make public our stance. She did nearly everything for me, including that.

I seldom met Father during the war. But one day he popped up and took me off to a party with his journalist friends. The glasses were standing ready, there were voices and laughter and the cigarette smoke was dense. I went round being introduced and answering questions. There was a relaxed and tolerant atmosphere and I could do what I wanted. I withdrew by myself and sidled along the bookshelves of this strange house.

I came across a newly published book called *The Martyrdom of Poland*. Documentary. I settled on the floor and read it just about cover to cover while the voices filled the air. That terrible book—which I have never seen again— contained what I feared, or perhaps what I hoped for. The Nazis were as inhuman as I had imagined, no, they were worse! I read fascinated and disturbed and at the same time a feeling of triumph emerged: I'd been right! It was all in the book, the proof was there. Just wait! One day this will be revealed, one day all of you who have doubted will have the truth thrown in your faces. Just wait! And that in the event is what happened.

LIBRARIES

"Medborgarhuset" (*lit.* "The Citizens' House") was built around 1940. A big four-square block in the middle of Söder, but also a bright and promising edifice, modern, "functional." It was only five minutes from where we lived.

In it there were, among other things, a public swimming pool and a branch of the city library. The children's section was, by obvious natural necessity, my allotted sphere, and to begin with it did have books enough for my consumption. The most important was Brehm's *Lives of the Animals*.

I slipped into the library nearly every day. But this was not an entirely trouble-free process. It sometimes happened that I tried to borrow books which the library ladies did not consider suitable for my age. One was Knut Holmboe's violent documentary *The Desert Is Burning*.

"Who is to have this book?"

"I am . . ."

"Oh no . . ."

"I . . ."

"You can tell your dad he can come and borrow it himself."

It was even worse when I tried to get into the adult section. I needed a book which was definitely not to be found in the children's section. I was stopped at the entrance.

"How old are you?"

"Eleven."

"You can't borrow books here. You can come back in a few years."

"Yes, but the book I want is only in here."

"What book?"

"*The Animals of Scandinavia: A History of Their Migration.*" And I added "by Ekman," in hollow tones, feeling the game was lost. It was. Out of the question. I blushed. I was furious. I would never forgive her!

In the meantime my uncle of few words—Uncle Elof—intervened. He gave me his card to the adult section and we maintained the fiction that I was collecting books for him. I could now get in where I wanted.

The adult section shared a wall with the pool. At the entry one felt the fumes from within, the chlorine smell came through the ventilation system and the echoing voices could be heard as from a distance. Swimming pools and suchlike always have strange acoustics. The temple of health and the temple of books were neighbours, a good idea. I was a faithful visitor to the Medborgarhus branch of the city library for many years. I regarded it as clearly superior to the central library up on Sveavägen—where the atmosphere was heavier and the air was still, no fumes of chlorine, no echoing voices. The books themselves had a different smell there; it gave me headaches.

Once given a free run of the library I devoted my attention mostly to nonfiction. I left literature to its fate. Likewise the shelves marked Economics and Social Problems. History, though, was interesting. Medicine scared me.

But it was Geography that was my favourite corner. I was a special devotee of the Africa shelf, which was extensive. I can recall titles like *Mount Elgon, A Market-Boy in Africa, Desert Sketches* . . . I wonder if any of the books which then filled the shelf are still there.

Someone called Albert Schweitzer had written a book enticingly called *Between Water and Primeval Forest*. It consisted mostly of speculations about life. But Schweitzer himself stayed put in his mission and didn't move, he wasn't a proper explorer. Not like, for instance, Gösta Moberg, who covered endless miles (why?) in alluring, unknown regions, such as Niger or Chad, lands about which there was scant information in the library. Kenya and "Tanganyika" however were favoured on account of their Swedish settlements. Tourists who sailed up the Nile to the Sudd area and then turned north again—they wrote books. But none of those who ventured into the arid zones of the Sudan, none of those who made their way into Kordofan or Dar Fur. The Portuguese colonies of Angola and Mozambique, that looked so big on the map, were also unknown and neglected areas on the Africa shelf—and that made them even more attractive.

I read a lot of books standing there in the library—I didn't want to take home too many books of the same kind, or the same book several times in succession. I felt I would be criticized by one or other of the library staff and that was something to be avoided at all costs.

One summer—I don't remember which one—I lived through an elaborate and persistent daydream about Africa. That was out on the island of Runmarö, a long way from the library. I withdrew into a fantasy—I was leading an expedition right through central Africa. I trudged on through the woods of Runmarö and kept track of roughly how far I'd gone with a dotted line on a big map of Africa, a map of the whole of Africa which I had drawn. If I worked out, for instance, that in the course of a week I had walked 120 kilometres on Runmarö, I marked in 120 kilometres on the map. It wasn't much.

At first I'd thought of starting the expedition on the east coast, more or less where Stanley had begun. But that would have left much too great a distance to traverse before I could reach the most interesting parts. I changed my mind and imagined that I travelled as far as Albert Nyansa by car. And that was where the expedition proper started, on foot. I would then have at least a reasonable chance of putting most of the Ituri Forest behind me before summer ended.

It was a nineteenth-century expedition, with bearers, etc. I was half aware, though, that this was now an obsolete way of travelling. Africa had changed. There was war in British Somaliland; it was in the news. Tanks were in action. It was indeed the first area where the Allies could claim an advance—I took due note of that, of course—and Abyssinia was the first country to be liberated from the Axis Powers.

When my Africa dream returned several years later, it had been modernized and was now almost realistic. I was thinking of becoming an entomologist and collecting insects in Africa, discovering new species instead of new deserts.

GRAMMAR SCHOOL

Only a couple of my classmates from primary school progressed to secondary school ("realskola"). And no one apart from myself applied to Södra Latin Grammar School.

There was an entrance exam I had to sit. My sole memory of that is that I spelled the word "särskilt" ("especially") wrongly, I gave it two l's. From then on the word had a disturbing effect on me which persisted far into the 1960s.

I have a distinct memory of my first day at Södra Latin in the autumn of 1942. It is as follows. I find myself surrounded by a number of unknown eleven-year-old boys. I have butterflies in my stomach, I'm uncertain and alone. But some of the others seem to know each other well—those are the pupils from Maria Preparatory. I look and look for a face from Katarina Norra. My mood consists of about equal parts of gloomy unease and hopeful expectation.

Our names are called out and we are divided into three classes. I am assigned to Class 15B and told to follow Dr. Mohlin, who is to be our class teacher. One of the oldest teachers. His subject is German. He is small, with a sort of catlike authority. He moves swiftly and quietly, he has bristly, reluctantly greying hair, and a bald wedge above each temple. From someone nearby who seems to know him, I catch an assessment of him: Målle—as he is called—is "strict but fair." Ominous.

From the first moment it was clear that grammar school was something quite different from primary school. Södra Latin was throughout masculine, the school was as single-sexed as a monastery or barracks. It was not until several years later that a couple of women were smuggled into the staff.

Each morning we all assembled in the school hall, sang hymns, and listened to a sermon delivered by one of the religious studies teachers. Then we marched off to our respective classrooms. The collective atmosphere of Södra Latin was immortalized by Ingmar Bergman in his film *Hets*.[1] (It was shot in the school and those of us who were pupils then appear as extras in several parts of the film.)

We were all supplied with a school manual which included, among other items, "Directives as to order and discipline, in accordance with the school's statues":

> The pupils shall attend instruction at the determined times, neatly and decently attired and in possession of the necessary textbooks. They shall observe good order and proper conduct and shall follow the instruction with due attention. The pupils shall likewise attend morning devotions and there deport themselves quietly and attentively . . .
>
> Pupils shall give due respect and obedience to the staff of the institution and shall accept with compliance their commands, corrections, and chastisements . . .

Södra Latin occupied the highest site on Söder, and its playground formed a plateau above most of the district's rooftops. The bricks of the school building could be seen from far away. The route to this castle of sighs was one I generally completed at a half-run. I hurried along by the long piles of wood—a sign of the crisis years—in front of "Björns Trädgård," made my way up Götgatan — past Hansson and Bruce's bookshop—swung to the left into Höbergsgatan and there, every winter morning, stood a horse chewing straw in a nose bag. It was a brewery horse, a big steaming Ardenne. For a moment I found myself in its reeking shadow and the memory of that patient beast and of its smell in the cold and damp is still vivid. A smell that was at once suffocating and comforting.

I would rush into the playground just as the bells began to summon us to morning service. I was hardly ever late, for everything between the hours of eight and nine in the morning was well-timed. The spring was firm and tense as the school day began.

---

1. *Hets*—in Britain the film was called *Frenzy* and in the USA *Torment*.

The end of the day at school was of course more relaxed, less regulated. Sometimes I went home with Palle. He was my closest friend in my first year at Södra Latin. We had quite a lot in common: his father, a sailor, was absent for long periods, and he was the only child of a good-natured mother who seemed pleased to see me. Palle had developed many of the characteristics of a single child, as I had, and he lived for his interests. He was above all a collector. Of what? Anything. Beer labels, matchboxes, swords, flint axes, stamps, postcards, shells, ethnographic oddments, and bones.

In his home, which was crammed full of his booty, we would duel with the swords. Together we carried out excavations at a secret spot on Riddarholmen and managed to retrieve bits of skeleton which my dentist identified as "parts of a human being."

Having Palle as a friend was an enriching experience but gradually we drifted apart. Further on in school Palle came to be absent for long periods because of illness. When he was transferred to another class we lost touch. My old friend was very far away. In fact he was marked by death. He appeared at school now only occasionally, pale and serious, with one leg amputated. When he died I found it impossible to accept. I developed a bad conscience but refused to recognize it. It felt as if I ought to suppress the memory of all the fun we'd had.

I feel I'm the same age as Palle, who died forty-five years ago without having grown up. But my old teachers, the "oldies" as they were collectively termed, remain old in my memory in spite of the fact that the older among them were about the same age as I am now as I write this. We always feel younger than we are. I carry inside myself my earlier faces, as a tree contains its rings. The sum of them is "me." The mirror sees only my latest face, while I know all my previous ones.

The teachers who stand out in my memory are of course those who generated tension or excitement, those who were vivid, colourful, original. They were not in the majority but there was a fair number of them. There was something tragic about some of them, which we were able to sense. A critical situation which could be described thus: "I know I can't be loved by those enviable turnip-heads in front of me. I know I can't be loved but at least I can make sure I won't be forgotten!"

The classroom was a theatre. The leading player, the teacher, performed on the stage, subjected to merciless scrutiny. The pupils were the audience and sometimes—one at a time— they would act a part as well.

We had to be on our guard, unfailingly. I had to get used to the recurring outbursts of aggression. Miss R had laid a good foundation—she had been strict and heavy-handed. Yet not really theatrical. At home there was nothing for me to learn in that direction. There were virtually no scenes at home, no rows, no bellowing father figure. Mother was spontaneous but undramatic. Giving vent to anger was childish. I had often been furious as a child but now I was a reasonably balanced youngster. My ideals were English—a stiff upper lip and so on. Outbursts of rage belonged to the Axis Powers.

At school there were choleric prima donnas who could devote most of a lesson to building up a tower of hysterical indignation, with the sole purpose of then emptying their vessels of wrath.

My class teacher Målle was hardly a prima donna. But he was the victim of a periodical and irresistible fury. Målle was really a charming person and a good teacher in his more harmonious periods. But, unhappily, what I remember best is that fury. Possibly the more violent outbursts did not come more often than three or four times a month. But it was upon those occasions that his great authority undoubtedly rested.

In the course of such lessons the thunder rolled to and fro across the landscape. That lightning would strike was clear to everyone, but no one could predict where. Målle did not victimize certain pupils. He was "strict but fair." Anyone might be struck by the lightning.

One day the lightning struck me. We were told to open our German grammars. I couldn't find mine. Was it in my schoolbag? Forgotten at home? I was lost. I couldn't find it.

"Stand up!"

I saw Målle dancing down from his desk and closing in on me. It was like being out in a field watching a bull approach.

The cuffs rained on me. I staggered this way and that. The next moment Målle was back sitting at his desk, frothing with rage, writing out a note for home. It was worded rather vaguely, accusing me of having been "careless during a lesson" or something like that.

Many of the teachers hoped that those written notes home would lead to interrogation and the infliction of further punishments at the hands of parents.

Not so with us. Mother listened to my story, took the note and signed it. She noticed then that I had blue marks on my face, caused by the ringed hand of the pedagogue. Her reaction was unexpectedly strong. She said she would contact the school, perhaps ring the headmaster.

To which I protested. She couldn't do that! Everything had turned out OK. But now "scandal" threatened. I would be called a mummy's boy and then persecuted forever, not just by Målle but by the entire staff.

She dropped the idea of course. And throughout my school days I made a point of keeping the two worlds—of school and of home—apart. If the two worlds were to seep into each other, then home would feel polluted. I would no longer have any proper refuge. Even today I find something disagreeable in the phrase "cooperation between home and school." I can see also that this holding apart of the separate worlds which I practiced gave rise in due course to a more deliberately maintained distinction between private life and society. (This has nothing to do with political inclinations, whether to the left or to the right.) What we live through in school is projected as an image of society. My total experience of school was mixed, with more darkness than light. Just as my image of society has become. (Although we could well ask what we mean by "society.")

Contact between teacher and pupil was intensely personal and important personal characteristics were magnified in the classroom atmosphere as the result of the many tense situations. Personal, yes, but not in the slightest private. We knew virtually nothing about the private lives of our teachers although most of them lived in the streets around the school. There were, naturally, rumours—e.g., that Målle had been a light-weight boxer in his youth—but they were feebly supported by proper evidence and we scarcely gave them credit. We had trustworthy information about two of the most discreet younger teachers, men who never inspired any drama. One of them, allegedly, was poor and eked out his salary by playing the piano in a restaurant in the evenings. He had been seen. The other, allegedly, was a chess champion. That had been in the newspaper.

One day in the autumn Målle came into a lesson with a *Russula aerugina* in his hand. He set the mushroom on his desk. It was both liberating and shocking to have caught a glimpse of his private life! We knew now that Målle gathered mushrooms.

None of the teachers expressed political opinions. But at that time there were of course unprecedented tensions in the staff room. The Second World War was being fought out there too. Many of the teachers were convinced Nazis. As late as 1944 one of them, it was said, exclaimed in the staff room, "If Hitler falls then *I* shall fall!" He didn't fall, however. I had him in German later. He recovered so well that he was able to welcome Hesse's Nobel Prize in 1946 with triumphant bellowing.

I was a worthy pupil but not one of the best. Biology ought to have been my favourite subject, but for most of my secondary schooling I had a biology teacher who really was too odd. At some point in the past he had blotted his copybook hopelessly, he had been warned and was now like a quenched volcano. My best subjects were geography and history. There I had an assistant teacher called Brännman, ruddy, energetic, a youngish man whose straight blond hair had a tendency to stand on end when he got angry, which happened quite often. He had plenty of goodwill and I liked him. The essays I wrote were always on geographical or historical subjects. They were long. On that point I heard a story much later from another Södra Latin pupil, Bo Grandien.[2] Bo became a close friend of mine in the later years of school but what he told me related to an earlier year when we didn't know each other.

He said that the first time he heard me mentioned was as he passed some of my classmates in one of the breaks. They had just been given back their essays and were dissatisfied with their grades. Bo heard the indignant remark: "We can't ALL write AS FAST as Tranan, can we?"[3]

Bo decided that "Tranan" was a detestable character who ought to be avoided. To me, this story is in a way comforting. Nowadays well known for deficient productivity, I was then clearly noted as a prolific scribbler, someone who sinned through excessive productivity, a literal Stakhanov.

EXORCISM

During the winter when I was fifteen I was afflicted by a severe form of anxiety. I was trapped by a searchlight which radiated not light but darkness. I was caught each afternoon as twilight fell and not released from that terrible grip until next day dawned. I slept very little, I sat up in bed, usually with a thick book before me. I read several thick books in that period but I can't say I really read them for they left no trace in my memory. The books were a pretext for leaving the light on.

It began in late autumn. One evening I'd gone to the cinema and seen *Squandered Days*, a film about an alcoholic. He finishes in a state of delirium—

---

2. Poet and journalist (b. 1932).
3. "Tranan": the crane (the bird).

a harrowing sequence which today I would perhaps find rather childish. But not then.

As I lay down to sleep I reran the film in my mind's eye, as one does after being at the cinema.

Suddenly the atmosphere in the room was tense with dread. Something took total possession of me. Suddenly my body started shaking, especially my legs. I was a clockwork toy which had been wound up and now rattled and jumped helplessly. The cramps were quite beyond the control of my will, I had never experienced anything like this. I screamed for help and Mother came through. Gradually the cramps ebbed out. And did not return. But my dread intensified and from dusk to dawn would not leave me alone. The feeling that dominated my nights was the terror which Fritz Lang came near to catching in certain scenes of *Dr. Mabuse's Testament*, especially the opening scene—a print works where someone hides while the machines and everything else vibrate. I recognized myself in this immediately, although my nights were quieter.

The most important element in my existence was *Illness*. The world was a vast hospital. I saw before me human beings deformed in body and in soul. The light burned and tried to hold off the terrible faces but sometimes I would doze off, my eyelids would close, and the terrible faces would suddenly be closing in on me.

It all happened in silence, yet within the silence voices were endlessly busy. The wallpaper pattern made faces. Now and then the silence would be broken by a ticking in the walls. Produced by what? By whom? By me? The walls crackled because my sick thoughts wanted them to. So much the worse. . . . Was I insane? Almost.

I was afraid of drifting into madness but in general I did not feel threatened by any kind of illness—it was scarcely a case of hypochondria—but it was rather the total power of illness that aroused terror. As in a film where an innocuous apartment interior changes its character entirely when ominous music is heard, I now experienced the outer world quite differently because it included my awareness of that domination wielded by sickness. A few years previously I had wanted to be an explorer. Now I had pushed my way into an unknown country where I had never wanted to be. I had discovered an evil power. Or rather, the evil power had discovered me.

I read recently about some teenagers who lost all their joy in living because they became obsessed with the idea that AIDS had taken over the world. They would have understood me.

Mother had witnessed the cramps I suffered that evening in late autumn as my crisis began. But after that she had to be held outside it all. Everyone had to be excluded, what was going on was just too terrible to be talked about. I was surrounded by ghosts. I myself was a ghost. A ghost that walked to school every morning and sat through the lessons without revealing its secret. School had become a breathing space, my dread wasn't the same there. It was my private life that was haunted. Everything was upside down.

At that time I was skeptical towards all forms of religion and I certainly said no prayers. If the crisis had arisen a few years later I would have been able to experience it as a revelation, something that would rouse me, like Siddhartha's four encounters (with an old person, with a sick person, with a corpse, and with a begging monk). I would have managed to feel a little more sympathy for and a little less dread of the deformed and the sick who invaded my nocturnal consciousness. But then, caught in my dread, religiously coloured explanations were not available to me. No prayers, but attempts at exorcism by way of music. It was during that period I began to hammer at the piano in earnest.

And all the time I was growing. At the beginning of that autumn term I was one of the smallest in the class, but by its end I was one of the tallest. As if the dread I lived in were a kind of fertilizer helping the plant to shoot up.

Winter moved towards its end and the days lengthened. Now, miraculously, the darkness in my own life withdrew. It happened gradually and I was slow in realizing fully what was happening. One spring evening I discovered that all my terrors were now marginal. I sat with some friends philosophizing and smoking cigars. It was time to walk home through the pale spring night and I had no feeling at all of terrors waiting for me there.

Still, it is something I have taken part in. Possibly my most important experience. But it came to an end. I thought it was Inferno but it was Purgatory.

III

AS WHEN YOU WERE A CHILD

As when you were a child and some tremendous hurt
was pulled over your head like a sack—
glints of sunshine through the mesh
and the hum of the cherry trees.

But it doesn't help, the great hurt
covers head and torso and knees
and though you are able to move sometimes
spring brings no happiness.

Yes, shimmering wool cap, pull it down over your face
stare through the mesh.
Out on the bay, the rings of water multiply soundlessly.
Green leaves darken the earth.

APRIL AND SILENCE

Spring lies deserted.
The dark velvet ditch
creeps by my side
not reflecting anything.

All that shines
are yellow flowers.

I am carried in my shadow
like a violin
in its black case.

All I want to say
gleams out of reach
like the silver
in a pawnshop.

NIGHT BOOK PAGE

I landed one night in May
in chilly moonlight
where grass and flowers were gray
but the smell green.

I glided up the hillside
in the color-blind night
while white stones
signaled to the moon.

A time in space
a few minutes long,
fifty-eight years wide.

And behind me
beyond the water gleaming like lead
was the other coast
and the ones who ruled.

People with futures
instead of faces.

THREE STANZAS

I

The knight and his lady
turned to stone but happy
on a flying coffin-lid
outside time.

II

Jesus held up a coin
with Tiberius in profile
a profile without love
power in circulation.

III

A dripping sword
wipes out the memories.
On the ground trumpets
and sword-belts rust.

LANDSCAPE WITH SUNS

The sun slides out from behind the house
stands in the middle of the street
and breathes on us
with its red wind.
Innsbrück I must leave you.
But tomorrow
there will be a glowing sun
in the half-dead grey forest
where we shall work and live.

FROM JULY —90

It was a funeral
and I felt that the dead man
read my thoughts
better than I could.

The organ was silent, the birds sang.
The pit out in the sunshine.
My friend's voice resided
on the far side of the minutes.

I drove home seen through
by the glitter of the summer-day,
by the rain and stillness,
seen through by the moon.

LEAFLET

The silent rage scribbles on the walls within.
Fruit trees in bloom, the cuckoo calls.
It's the anaesthesia of spring. But the silent rage
Paints its slogans backwards in the garage.

We see everything and nothing, but upright like periscopes
handled by the underworld's shy crew.
It's the war of the minutes. The blazing sun
stands above the hospital, suffering's parking place.

We living nails hammered down in society!
One day we'll come loose from everything.
We'll feel the wind of death under our wings
and become milder and wilder than here.

THE CUCKOO

A cuckoo sat and called in the birch just north of the house.
Its voice was so powerful that at first I thought it
was an opera singer performing a cuckoo imitation. Surprised
I saw the bird. Its tailfeathers moved up and down with each
note like a pump-handle at a well. The bird hopped, turned
around and shouted to all four directions. Then it lifted into the air
and flew cursing under its breath over the house and far off into the West . . .
The summer grows old and everything flows together into a single
melancholy whisper. Cuculus canorus returns to the tropics. Its time in Sweden
is over. It wasn't long! As a matter of fact the cuckoo is a citizen of Zaire. . .
I am no longer so fond of travelling. But the journey visits me.
Now that I am being pushed further into a corner, now that the annual
rings widen and I need reading-glasses. Always what happens is more
than we can carry! There is nothing to be astonished about. These
thoughts carry me just as loyally as Susi and Chuma carried Livingstone's
mummified body straight through Africa.

TWO CITIES

On their own sides of a channel, two cities,
one blacked out, occupied by the enemy.
In the other the lamps are burning.
The bright shore hypnotises the one in darkness.

I swim out in a trance
on the glittering dark water.
A muffled blast from a tuba presses in on me.
It's a friend's voice, take your grave and go.

AFTER A VISIT TO THE DDR

The almighty cyclop's-eye clouded over
and the grass shook itself in the coal dust.

Beaten black and blue by the night's dreams
we board the train
that stops at every station
and lays eggs.

Almost silent.
The clang of the church bells' buckets
fetching water.
And someone's inexorable cough
scolding everything and everyone.

A stone idol moves its lips:
it's the city.
Ruled by iron-hard misunderstandings
among kiosk-attendants butchers metal-workers naval officers
iron-hard misunderstandings, academics!

How sore my eyes are!
They have seen
they have read by the faint glimmer of the glow-worm lamps.

But we can hear the clang
of the church bells' buckets when they fetch water
every Wednesday
—is it Wednesday?—
so much for our Sundays!

AIR MAIL

I carried the letter through the city
in search of a mail box.
In the great forest of stone and concrete
fluttered that lost butterfly.

The stamp's flying carpet
the address's staggering letters
plus my sealed-in truth
at this moment floating above the ocean.

The Atlantic's crawling silver.
The banks of clouds. The fishing boat
like a spit-out olive pit.
And the pale scar of its wake.

Down here work goes slowly.
Often I steal a glance at the clock.
The shadows of the trees are black ciphers
in the greedy silence.

Truth is there on the ground
but no one dares to take it.
Truth lies on the street.
No one makes it his own.

NOCTURNAL JOURNEY

There is a rumbling beneath us. The trains are running.
Hotel Astoria trembles.
A glass of water at the edge of the bed
shines in the tunnels.

He dreamed he was a prisoner in Svalbard.
The planet rolled over rumbling.
Sparkling eyes walked over the ice.
It was there, the miracles' beauty.

A SKETCH FROM 1844

William Turner's face is brown from the weather,
he sets his easel far out in the breakers.
We follow the silver green cable down into the depths.

He wades out into the shallow kingdom of the dead.
A train rolls in. Come closer.
Rain, rain journeys over us.

EIGHT HAIKU

(May)

Power lines
taut in the kingdom of cold
north of all music.

The white sun
practices long distance running
against death's blue mountain

We must live
with the small print of the grass
and the cellar laughter.

The sun is low now.
Our shadows are giants.
Soon all will be shadow.

(June)

The orchids.
Tankers glide by.
Full moon.

(July)

Medieval fortress,
alien town, cold sphinx,
empty arenas.

The leaves whispered:
a wild boar plays the organ.
And the bells tolled.

And the night streams
from East to West with
the speed of the moon.

THE LIGHT STREAMS IN

Outside the window is the long beast of spring
the transparent dragon of sunlight
flows past like an endless
commuter train—we never got a glimpse of its head.

The waterfront villas move sideways
they are proud like crabs.
The sun makes the statues blink.

The raging sea of fire out in space
is transformed on earth to a caress.
The countdown has begun.

ISLAND LIFE, 1860

I

Down at the dock she was washing clothes one day,
and the deepsea cold rose right up along her arms
and into her being.

Her frozen tears became spectacles.
The island lifted itself by its own grass
and the herring flag floated far down in the sea.

II

Also the swarming hive of smallpox got to him
settled onto his face.
He lies in bed looking at the ceiling.

How hard it is to row up the stream of silence.
This moment's stain that flows out for eternity
this moment's wound that bleeds in for eternity.

WITHIN THE WALLS IS ENDLESSNESS

1827. Spring. Beethoven
hoists his death mask and sails away.

The windmills of Europe grind.
The wild geese fly to the north.

Here is north, here is Stockholm
floating palaces and hovels.

The logs in the royal fireplace
sag from Attention to At Ease.

Peace prevails, vaccine and potatoes,
but the city's wells breathe heavily.

Shit barrels borne like pashas
through the night over North Bridge.

Mam'sels, tramps, and fine gentlemen,
the cobblestones make them stagger.

Implacably still is the signboard
with the smoking blackamoor.

So many islands, so much rowing
with invisible oars against the current.

The channels open, April, May
and soft, honey dribbling June.

Heat reaches the far islands.
The village doors, all but one, open.

The snake clock's pointers lick the silence.
The stony banks shine with geologic patience.

This is the way it happened, or almost.
It's a shadowy family story

of Eric, cast under a spell,
invalid with a bullet through his soul.

On a journey to the city he met an enemy
and sailed home sick and gray.

That summer he took to his bed.
On the walls his tools grieve.

He lies awake, hears the night moths,
wooly flutterings of his moonlight companions.

His strength dwindles, he presses in vain
against the iron clad approaching day.

And the God of the depths cries out from the depths,
"Deliver me! Deliver yourself!"

All that happens without, turns within.
He's pulled to pieces, he's gathered up.

The wind rises and the wild rose bushes
catch at the escaping light.

The future opens out, he looks into
the self-revolving kaleidoscope,

sees the indistinct, fluttering faces
of future generations.

By mistake I meet his glance
as I walk around here

among Washington's houses of power,
where only every other pillar holds.

White buildings in the style of crematoriums
where the dreams of the poor turn to ashes.

The gentle slope begins to steepen,
and before you notice it's become an abyss.

VERMEER

It's not a sheltered world. The noise begins over there, on the other side of
    the wall
where the alehouse is
with its laughter and quarrels, its rows of teeth, its tears, its chiming of
    clocks,
and the psychotic brother-in-law, the murderer, in whose presence everyone
    feels fear.

The huge explosion and the emergency crew arriving late,
boats showing off on the canals, money slipping down into pockets—the
    wrong man's—
ultimatum piled on ultimatum,
wide-mouthed red flowers whose sweat reminds us of approaching war.

And then straight through the wall—from there—straight into the airy
    studio
and the seconds that have got permission to live for centuries.
Paintings that choose the name: "The Music Lesson"
or "A Woman in Blue Reading a Letter."
She is eight months pregnant, two hearts beating inside her.
The wall behind her holds a crinkly map of Terra Incognita.

Just breathe. An unidentifiable blue fabric has been tacked to the chairs.
Gold-headed tacks flew in with astronomical speed
and stopped smack there
as if they had always been stillness and nothing else.

The ears experience a buzz, perhaps it's depth or perhaps height.
It's the pressure from the other side of the wall,
the pressure that makes each fact float
and makes the brushstroke firm.

Passing through walls hurts human beings, they get sick from it,
but we have no choice.
It's all one world. Now to the walls.
The walls are a part of you.
One either knows that, or one doesn't; but it's the same for everyone
except for small children. There aren't any walls for them.

The airy sky has taken its place leaning against the wall.
It is like a prayer to what is empty.
And what is empty turns its face to us
and whispers:
'I am not empty, I am open.'

ABOUT THE AUTHOR

Tomas Tranströmer was born in Stockholm in 1931. He is a psychologist by profession and worked from 1960 to 1966 at Roxtuna Prison for Boys. Since 1967 he has worked with the occupationally handicapped in Västerås. One of Sweden's most distinguished poets, he has received the prestigious Bonnier poetry prize and the Petrarch Prize. He lives in Västerås, 40 miles west of Stockholm, with his wife, Monica.